Counting

by Alex Oncley

Companion to **Ice For Sale**

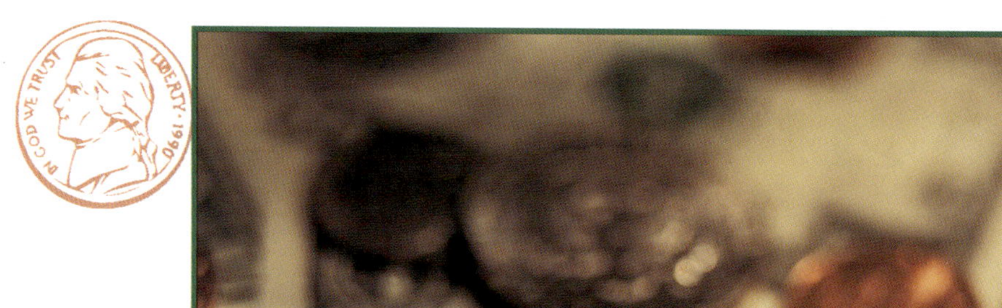

You use money every day.
Money can be coins or bills.
Each coin or bill has its own value.

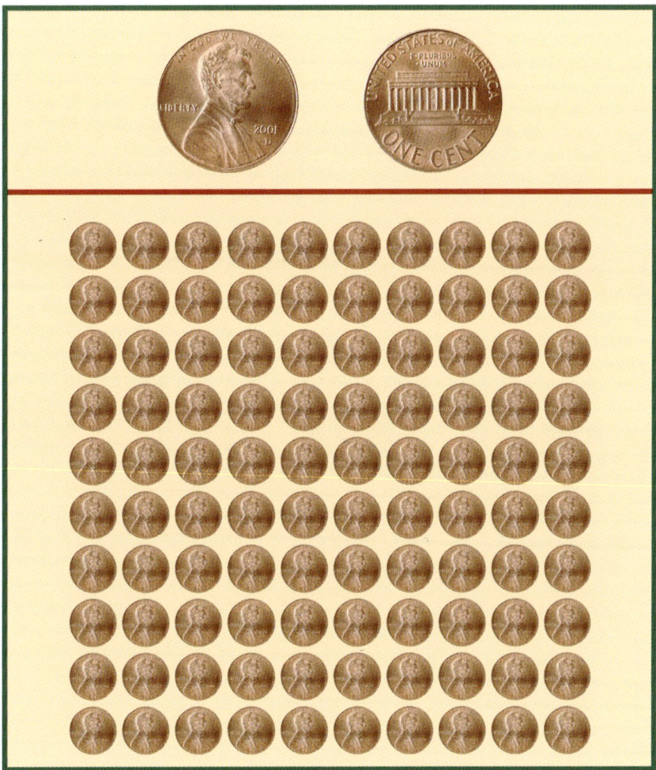

A penny is worth 1 cent.
That's not much.
But 100 pennies equal a dollar.

=

A nickel is worth 5 cents.
It is equal to 5 pennies.

 =  

A dime is worth 10 cents.
It is equal to 2 nickels.

A quarter is worth 25 cents.
It is equal to 5 nickels.
It also equals 2 dimes and 1 nickel.

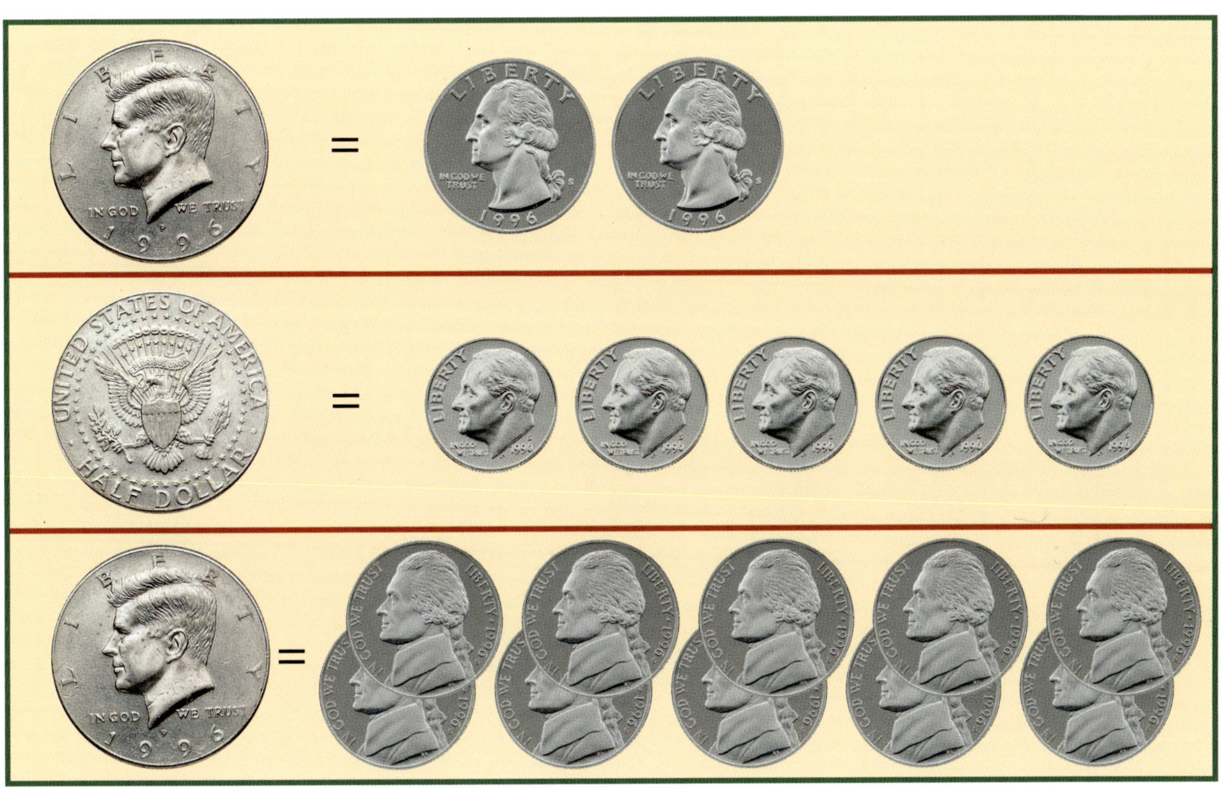

A half-dollar is worth 50 cents.
It is equal to 2 quarters, 5 dimes,
or 10 nickels.

A dollar can be a bill or a coin.

You can add coins in different ways to make the same amount of money. Tara needs 65 cents.

25¢ + 25¢ + 10¢ + 5¢ = 65¢

Here's one way to make 65 cents:
quarter + quarter + dime +
nickel = 65¢

10¢ + 10¢ + 10¢ +

10¢ + 10¢ + 10¢ + 5¢ = 65¢

Here's another way:
dime + dime + dime +
dime + dime + dime + nickel = 65¢

How many ways can you make $1.00?

Use these coins:

pennies nickels

dimes quarters

half-dollars